2011

January
S	M	T	W	T	F	S
						1
2	3	4	5	6	7	8
9	10	11	12	13	14	15
16	17	18	19	20	21	22
23	24	25	26	27	28	29
30	31					

February
S	M	T	W	T	F	S
		1	2	3	4	5
6	7	8	9	10	11	12
13	14	15	16	17	18	19
20	21	22	23	24	25	26
27	28					

March
S	M	T	W	T	F	S
		1	2	3	4	5
6	7	8	9	10	11	12
13	14	15	16	17	18	19
20	21	22	23	24	25	26
27	28	29	30	31		

April
S	M	T	W	T	F	S
					1	2
3	4	5	6	7	8	9
10	11	12	13	14	15	16
17	18	19	20	21	22	23
24	25	26	27	28	29	30

May
S	M	T	W	T	F	S
1	2	3	4	5	6	7
8	9	10	11	12	13	14
15	16	17	18	19	20	21
22	23	24	25	26	27	28
29	30	31				

June
S	M	T	W	T	F	S
			1	2	3	4
5	6	7	8	9	10	11
12	13	14	15	16	17	18
19	20	21	22	23	24	25
26	27	28	29	30		

July
S	M	T	W	T	F	S
					1	2
3	4	5	6	7	8	9
10	11	12	13	14	15	16
17	18	19	20	21	22	23
24	25	26	27	28	29	30
31						

August
S	M	T	W	T	F	S
	1	2	3	4	5	6
7	8	9	10	11	12	13
14	15	16	17	18	19	20
21	22	23	24	25	26	27
28	29	30	31			

September
S	M	T	W	T	F	S
				1	2	3
4	5	6	7	8	9	10
11	12	13	14	15	16	17
18	19	20	21	22	23	24
25	26	27	28	29	30	

October
S	M	T	W	T	F	S
						1
2	3	4	5	6	7	8
9	10	11	12	13	14	15
16	17	18	19	20	21	22
23	24	25	26	27	28	29
30	31					

November
S	M	T	W	T	F	S
		1	2	3	4	5
6	7	8	9	10	11	12
13	14	15	16	17	18	19
20	21	22	23	24	25	26
27	28	29	30			

December
S	M	T	W	T	F	S
				1	2	3
4	5	6	7	8	9	10
11	12	13	14	15	16	17
18	19	20	21	22	23	24
25	26	27	28	29	30	31

2012

January
S	M	T	W	T	F	S
1	2	3	4	5	6	7
8	9	10	11	12	13	14
15	16	17	18	19	20	21
22	23	24	25	26	27	28
29	30	31				

February
S	M	T	W	T	F	S
			1	2	3	4
5	6	7	8	9	10	11
12	13	14	15	16	17	18
19	20	21	22	23	24	25
26	27	28	29			

March
S	M	T	W	T	F	S
				1	2	3
4	5	6	7	8	9	10
11	12	13	14	15	16	17
18	19	20	21	22	23	24
25	26	27	28	29	30	31

April
S	M	T	W	T	F	S
1	2	3	4	5	6	7
8	9	10	11	12	13	14
15	16	17	18	19	20	21
22	23	24	25	26	27	28
29	30					

May
S	M	T	W	T	F	S
		1	2	3	4	5
6	7	8	9	10	11	12
13	14	15	16	17	18	19
20	21	22	23	24	25	26
27	28	29	30	31		

June
S	M	T	W	T	F	S
					1	2
3	4	5	6	7	8	9
10	11	12	13	14	15	16
17	18	19	20	21	22	23
24	25	26	27	28	29	30

July
S	M	T	W	T	F	S
1	2	3	4	5	6	7
8	9	10	11	12	13	14
15	16	17	18	19	20	21
22	23	24	25	26	27	28
29	30	31				

August
S	M	T	W	T	F	S
			1	2	3	4
5	6	7	8	9	10	11
12	13	14	15	16	17	18
19	20	21	22	23	24	25
26	27	28	29	30	31	

September
S	M	T	W	T	F	S
						1
2	3	4	5	6	7	8
9	10	11	12	13	14	15
16	17	18	19	20	21	22
23	24	25	26	27	28	29
30						

October
S	M	T	W	T	F	S
	1	2	3	4	5	6
7	8	9	10	11	12	13
14	15	16	17	18	19	20
21	22	23	24	25	26	27
28	29	30	31			

November
S	M	T	W	T	F	S
				1	2	3
4	5	6	7	8	9	10
11	12	13	14	15	16	17
18	19	20	21	22	23	24
25	26	27	28	29	30	

December
S	M	T	W	T	F	S
						1
2	3	4	5	6	7	8
9	10	11	12	13	14	15
16	17	18	19	20	21	22
23	24	25	26	27	28	29
30	31					

The Bedford/ St. Martin's Planner

with Grammar Girl's Quick and Dirty Tips

Lois Hassan

Henry Ford Community College

BEDFORD/ST. MARTIN'S Boston ◆ New York

Manufactured in the United States of America.

For information, write: Bedford/St. Martin's, 75 Arlington Street, Boston, MA 02116 (617-399-4000)

ISBN-10: 0–312–60642–7
ISBN-13: 978–0–312–60642–8

Acknowledgments

Grammar Girl, Modern Manners Guy, and Quick and Dirty Tips are trademarks of Mignon Fogarty, Inc. Grammar Girl and Modern Manners Guy Tips copyright Mignon Fogarty, Inc. (used by permission). Get-It-Done Guy is a trademark of Macmillan Holdings, LLC. Get-It-Done Guy Tips copyright Macmillan Holdings, LLC (used by permission).

Contents

Getting Started

❝ Before everything else,
getting ready is the secret to success. ❞

—Henry Ford (1863–1947),
inventor and founder of Ford Motor Company

Introduction: Why Plan?

Imagine three separate households where three different students—Rick, Carmen, and Ava—are waking up to busy days: a job interview, followed by classes and other commitments. Rick and Carmen wrote out their plans for their days the night before. Let's take a look:

Rick		Carmen	
Tuesday:		**Tonight:**	
7 AM:	Get up and get ready.	Lay out and iron clothes. Reread materials for interview. Print out Google directions to Hart Building.	
9 AM:	Job interview at Flanders, Inc.	**Tuesday:**	
NOON:	Lunch with Alfredo.	*6 AM:*	Get up and get kids ready. Get dressed.
3–9 PM:	Work/class (test).	*7:30 AM:*	Drop kids off at day care; drive downtown.
		9–11 AM:	Job interview with Don Stingle at Hart Building downtown.
		11 AM–NOON:	Early lunch; review flash cards for test.
		NOON–2 PM:	Help Mom at store.
		2–3 PM:	Walk/exercise.
		3–4 PM:	Pick up groceries and get kids at daycare.
		4–6 PM:	Feed kids/self. Pick up Mom to watch kids. Review flash cards once again.
		7–9 PM:	Class (take test).
		9–11 PM:	Carmen time and bedtime!

Ava, on the other hand, figured that writing a plan would be a waste of time. She decided to get up at her usual time (an hour before her 9 AM job interview) and take it from there. She had a pretty good sense of the other things she had going on for the day, so she wasn't worried.

> **Now, you decide:** Who will be the most likely to make the most of his or her day and to do things on time? Rank the plans from Rick, Carmen, and Ava from 1 to 3, with 1 being the "most likely" and 3 being the "least likely."

Ava

There's a good chance you gave Ava's plan a 3. Will an hour be enough time for her to get ready for, and get to, her interview? Maybe, or maybe not. Also, she's relying on her memory to keep track of other commitments for the day. But will she remember that she has a test in her afternoon math class — a test for which she should set aside study time beforehand?

Rick and Carmen

Now, let's look at Rick's and Carmen's plans. Both of these students are at least a step ahead of Ava simply because they made plans. However, while Rick recorded all of his major commitments, his plans aren't very detailed. For instance, it appears that he has a test, but when does he plan to study for it? How does he plan to use his time after lunch? Probably, Rick's plan deserves a score of 2.

Carmen not only planned her busy Tuesday, she also plotted out what she needed to do the night before. For Tuesday, she wrote out her plans for every block of time, setting aside time for studying and specific chores, and even for exercise and "Carmen time." Because of its thoroughness, Carmen's plan deserves a score of 1.

Like many successful people with busy schedules, Carmen understands that if she doesn't make time for something, it isn't going to happen. If you have a vague idea that you'll study for a test sometime during a day, but you do not pick a specific time to devote to studying, it will be easy to fill your time with other things and never meet your goal.

. . . Now, You!

Becoming an effective planner isn't hard; it just takes commitment and a small investment of time. You have already taken an important first step by opening up this little booklet. On the following pages, you'll learn other simple steps to becoming more organized and "goal-oriented." And you'll be able to start making your plans right away with the schedules and calendars on pages 11–142.

At the end of this booklet, on pages 143–150 and the inside back cover, you'll find other handy resources—like studying advice, grammar help, and useful Web sites—to assist you in college. Make sure to keep this planner with you at all times, and check it throughout the day to stay on track!

Planning Is as Easy as 1, 2, 3 . . .

Following are the core planning tools in this booklet:

- The blank schedules starting on page 11.
- The monthly calendars starting on page 23.
- The weekly calendars starting on page 37.

Flip through these tools to familiarize yourself with them. Then, follow the steps below.

1. Keep a Schedule and a Calendar.

First, use the blank schedules to record time commitments that will stay the same across a semester or year: class times, work hours, day care drop-offs or pick-ups, regular meetings, meal times, gym times, and so on. We have provided a few copies in case your schedule changes or in case you want to make alternative schedules.

Then, turn to the weekly calendar that begins on page 37 and at the tops of the pages, record the months and week numbers for a year's time. (To do so, you can refer to the yearly calendars on the inside front cover of this planner.) Then, for each week, write in the days. (Notice that there is also a monthly calendar, starting on page 23. After you have filled in the weekly calendar, you may want to transfer important dates that you want to see "at a glance" to the monthly calendar.)

When you have finished preparing your weekly calendar, record the following in the appropriate days and time slots:

- Assignment due dates
- Other school and work deadlines
- Test dates/times
- Dates/times of conferences with instructors
- Other meeting dates/times
- Dates/times of medical appointments
- Bill due dates
- Social commitments
- Dates of birthdays, anniversaries, holidays, and other vacations or celebrations
- Any other important commitments that you do not want to forget

Quick and Dirty Tip from Modern Manners Guy™

Be courteous; be on time: Being on time not only makes it easier to make plans and coordinate schedules, but it shows others that you respect and value their time. If you are going to be more than five minutes late, call the person whom you are meeting and let him or her know where you are and when you'll arrive.

For a podcast on this subject, visit **manners.quickanddirtytips.com.** Topic: "Fashionably Late"

You might want to write tests, assignment due dates, and other especially important commitments in a different and bright color, like red. Or you might mark them with a bright highlighter. **Important academic dates are usually marked in your course syllabi, so be sure to refer to your syllabi as you add to your calendar.**

Now, **build in time to study!** Once you have filled in all of your commitments, fill in times to study. Ideally, you will record some "permanent" study times as part of your schedule.

To figure out how many hours a week to devote to studying, a good rule of thumb is to take your number of credit hours and multiply it by 2. Look at the following example:

15 credit hours x 2 = 30 hours of studying a week

Although it's great to have two or three hours at a time to study, this won't always be possible. If you can fit in a half hour during breakfast or even 15 minutes during a coffee break, it will be time well spent!

If you have some flexibility in terms of when you can study, consider this advice:

- Try to study right after class, when the information that you learned can be easily recalled.

- Try to study when you are most alert and ready to learn. Decide whether you work best in the morning, during the day, or in the evening, and plan your study time accordingly.

Some final, important notes:

- As soon as you learn of new commitments or changes to existing ones, write these in your calendar immediately.

- To prepare for each day, refer first to your schedule and then to the day's events on your calendar. (You might do this on the

---

Quick and Dirty Tip from Get-It-Done Guy™

Say no: Most of us have a hard time saying no, but if you say "yes" to more than you can handle, you'll never, ever catch up. When your plate is full, review and reprioritize tasks.

For a podcast on this subject, visit **getitdone.quickanddirtytips.com.**
Topic: "Overcommit? 'No' More"

previous evening or first thing in the morning.) Note the day's events and commitments and decide what preparations are necessary. Later in the day, check your schedule and calendar again to make sure that you're on track.

- If, through planning, you see that all your scheduled commitments leave you no time for studying and personal time, you may have to rethink your commitments. Do you need to consider cutting back on hours devoted to work and/or school? Can you make other adjustments? **Remember: An unrealistic plan is a worthless plan.**

2. Prioritize with a To-Do List.

With schedules and calendars, you assign dates and times to specific tasks and commitments to make sure you follow through on them.

With a to-do list, you write down everything that you want to accomplish on a specific day. Often, this list will overlap somewhat with a schedule or calendar. However, it's a good idea to keep a to-do list, apart from a schedule or calendar, so that you don't forget important daily steps in meeting your goals.

Remember Carmen, whose schedule was shown on page 2? Let's look at her to-do list for that same Tuesday:

To-Do List for Tuesday

Must-Do's

- Do final prep for job interview: Read company background information and review questions I want to ask and questions I might be asked.
- Do interview.
- Do final studying for test: Review flash cards and notes.
- Take test.

Try-to-Do's

- Write thank-you note to Don Stingle for job interview. (Must do by end of week!)
- Ask Mom if she needs help with insurance application.
- Ask Alvaro and Betsy if they can study with me next week.

To make your own to-do list, follow these steps:

1. As Carmen did, it's a good idea to **first list any activities that must be completed that day.** Follow these with activities that would be nice to complete but aren't musts for that day.

2. Check off or cross out each activity as you complete it. At the end of the day, reprioritize any activity not checked off, transferring it to a fresh to-do list.

3. If you have transferred the same activity ahead for two or more days, think about whether you really want to complete it. If you want to do it, do it first the next day. If you don't want to do it, don't do it, but remember that you will have to face the consequences if there are any.

You can write your to-do lists in a separate booklet that you keep with this planner. (You might even start your to-do lists in this planner, in the blank "notes" pages at the end of the planner.)

3. Don't Lose Sight of the Big Picture.

As you move busily through each day, don't lose sight of important long-term goals that you have for school, your professional life, and your personal life. Do you want to learn more about what nurses do before you decide whether to major in nursing? Do you want to find a better-paying part-time job? Do you want to learn how to kayak or play the drums?

Take some time to fill out the goal-setting worksheet that follows. Then, ask what first steps toward meeting these goals you might take now: scheduling an appointment to talk with a nurse from a local hospital? Updating your résumé? Looking into kayaking or drum lessons? Firm up these plans, add them to your calendar, and update and refine your plans over time.

Quick and Dirty Tip from Get-It-Done Guy™

Keep a traveling to-do list: Get a 3" x 5" spiral notepad, and keep it with you at all times to write down tasks that come up during the day. Later, transfer the items to a master to-do list. This process will force you to reconsider tasks and set priorities.

For a podcast on this subject, visit **getitdone.quickanddirtytips.com.** Topic: "To Do or Not To Do"

Goal-Setting Worksheet

Find a quiet place where you can concentrate and think about the goals you would like to achieve in your academic, work, and personal lives through this semester, this year, and over the next two years. Then, record your goals in the spaces provided.

Academic Goals

To Achieve by the End of This Semester

To Achieve By the End of this Academic Year

To Achieve within Two Years

Work Goals

To Achieve by the End of This Semester

To Achieve by the End of this Academic Year

To Achieve within Two Years

Personal Goals

To Achieve by the End of This Semester

To Achieve by the End of this Academic Year

To Achieve within Two Years

Quick and Dirty Tip from Modern Manners Guy™

Save time in the hallway: Have you ever asked the polite question "How are you?" and gotten someone's life story? Instead, you might greet a talkative acquaintance with something that offers less room for lengthy response. For instance, try "Hello, nice to see you," or simply "Hi, John," and offer him a smile as you pass by.

For a podcast on this subject, visit **manners.quickanddirtytips.com.** Topic: "How Are You?"

Schedules and Calendars

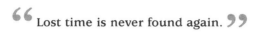 Lost time is never found again.

—Benjamin Franklin (1706–1790),
inventor and statesman

Schedule for _____

	Monday	Tuesday	Wednesday	Thursday	Friday	Saturday	Sunday
7 AM							
7:30							
8							
8:30							
9							
9:30							
10							
10:30							
11							
11:30							
Noon							
12:30 PM							
1							

1:30	2	2:30	3	3:30	4	4:30	5	5:30	6	6:30	7	7:30	8

Schedule for _____

	Monday	Tuesday	Wednesday	Thursday	Friday	Saturday	Sunday
7 AM							
7:30							
8							
8:30							
9							
9:30							
10							
10:30							
11							
11:30							
Noon							
12:30 PM							
1							

1:30							
2							
2:30							
3							
3:30							
4							
4:30							
5							
5:30							
6							
6:30							
7							
7:30							
8							

Schedule for _____

	Monday	Tuesday	Wednesday	Thursday	Friday	Saturday	Sunday
7 AM							
7:30							
8							
8:30							
9							
9:30							
10							
10:30							
11							
11:30							
Noon							
12:30 PM							
1							

1:30													
2													
2:30													
3													
3:30													
4													
4:30													
5													
5:30													
6													
6:30													
7													
7:30													
8													

SCHEDULES

18

Schedule for _____

	Monday	Tuesday	Wednesday	Thursday	Friday	Saturday	Sunday
7 AM							
7:30							
8							
8:30							
9							
9:30							
10							
10:30							
11							
11:30							
NOON							
12:30 PM							
1							

1:30	2	2:30	3	3:30	4	4:30	5	5:30	6	6:30	7	7:30	8

Schedule for _____

	Monday	Tuesday	Wednesday	Thursday	Friday	Saturday	Sunday
7 AM							
7:30							
8							
8:30							
9							
9:30							
10							
10:30							
11							
11:30							
Noon							
12:30 PM							
1							

1:30															
2															
2:30															
3															
3:30															
4															
4:30															
5															
5:30															
6															
6:30															
7															
7:30															
8															

Monthly Calendars

January

Sunday	Monday	Tuesday	Wednesday	Thursday	Friday	Saturday

February

Sunday	Monday	Tuesday	Wednesday	Thursday	Friday	Saturday

MONTH

March

Sunday	Monday	Tuesday	Wednesday	Thursday	Friday	Saturday

April

Sunday	Monday	Tuesday	Wednesday	Thursday	Friday	Saturday

MONTH

May

Sunday	Monday	Tuesday	Wednesday	Thursday	Friday	Saturday

June

Sunday	Monday	Tuesday	Wednesday	Thursday	Friday	Saturday

MONTH

July

Sunday	Monday	Tuesday	Wednesday	Thursday	Friday	Saturday

August

Sunday	Monday	Tuesday	Wednesday	Thursday	Friday	Saturday

MONTH

September

Sunday	Monday	Tuesday	Wednesday	Thursday	Friday	Saturday

October

Sunday	Monday	Tuesday	Wednesday	Thursday	Friday	Saturday

MONTH

November

Sunday	Monday	Tuesday	Wednesday	Thursday	Friday	Saturday

December

Sunday	Monday	Tuesday	Wednesday	Thursday	Friday	Saturday

MONTH

Weekly Calendars

Month(s) ————————————————————————

Monday the ————————

7 AM	2
8	3
9	4
10	5
11	6
NOON	7
1 PM	8

Tuesday the ————————

7 AM	2
8	3
9	4
10	5
11	6
NOON	7
1 PM	8

Wednesday the ————————

7 AM	2
8	3
9	4
10	5
11	6
NOON	7
1 PM	8

WEEK

Week No. _____

Thursday the _____

7 AM	2
8	3
9	4
10	5
11	6
NOON	7
1 PM	8

Friday the _____

7 AM	2
8	3
9	4
10	5
11	6
NOON	7
1 PM	8

Saturday the _____

7 AM	2
8	3
9	4
10	5
11	6
NOON	7
1 PM	8

Sunday the _____

7 AM	2
8	3
9	4
10	5
11	6
NOON	7
1 PM	8

WEEK

39

Month(s) _____

Monday the _____

7 AM	2
8	3
9	4
10	5
11	6
NOON	7
1 PM	8

Tuesday the _____

7 AM	2
8	3
9	4
10	5
11	6
NOON	7
1 PM	8

Wednesday the _____

7 AM	2
8	3
9	4
10	5
11	6
NOON	7
1 PM	8

Week No. _____

Thursday the _____

7 AM	2
8	3
9	4
10	5
11	6
Noon	7
1 PM	8

Friday the _____

7 AM	2
8	3
9	4
10	5
11	6
Noon	7
1 PM	8

Saturday the _____   Sunday the _____

7 AM	2	7 AM	2
8	3	8	3
9	4	9	4
10	5	10	5
11	6	11	6
Noon	7	Noon	7
1 PM	8	1 PM	8

WEEK

41

Month(s) ———————————————————

Monday the ——————————

7 AM	2
8	3
9	4
10	5
11	6
NOON	7
1 PM	8

Tuesday the ——————————

7 AM	2
8	3
9	4
10	5
11	6
NOON	7
1 PM	8

Wednesday the ——————————

7 AM	2
8	3
9	4
10	5
11	6
NOON	7
1 PM	8

WEEK

Week No. _____

Thursday the _____

7 AM	2
8	3
9	4
10	5
11	6
NOON	7
1 PM	8

Friday the _____

7 AM	2
8	3
9	4
10	5
11	6
NOON	7
1 PM	8

Saturday the _____ Sunday the _____

7 AM	2	7 AM	2
8	3	8	3
9	4	9	4
10	5	10	5
11	6	11	6
NOON	7	NOON	7
1 PM	8	1 PM	8

WEEK

43

Month(s) _____

Monday the _____

7 AM	2
8	3
9	4
10	5
11	6
NOON	7
1 PM	8

Tuesday the _____

7 AM	2
8	3
9	4
10	5
11	6
NOON	7
1 PM	8

Wednesday the _____

7 AM	2
8	3
9	4
10	5
11	6
NOON	7
1 PM	8

44

Week No. _____

Thursday the _____

7 AM	2
8	3
9	4
10	5
11	6
NOON	7
1 PM	8

Friday the _____

7 AM	2
8	3
9	4
10	5
11	6
NOON	7
1 PM	8

Saturday the _____

7 AM	2
8	3
9	4
10	5
11	6
NOON	7
1 PM	8

Sunday the _____

7 AM	2
8	3
9	4
10	5
11	6
NOON	7
1 PM	8

WEEK

Month(s) _____

Monday the _____

7 AM	*2*
8	*3*
9	*4*
10	*5*
11	*6*
NOON	*7*
1 PM	*8*

Tuesday the _____

7 AM	*2*
8	*3*
9	*4*
10	*5*
11	*6*
NOON	*7*
1 PM	*8*

Wednesday the _____

7 AM	*2*
8	*3*
9	*4*
10	*5*
11	*6*
NOON	*7*
1 PM	*8*

WEEK

46

Week No. _____

Thursday the _____

7 AM	2
8	3
9	4
10	5
11	6
NOON	7
1 PM	8

Friday the _____

7 AM	2
8	3
9	4
10	5
11	6
NOON	7
1 PM	8

Saturday the _____ Sunday the _____

7 AM	2	7 AM	2
8	3	8	3
9	4	9	4
10	5	10	5
11	6	11	6
NOON	7	NOON	7
1 PM	8	1 PM	8

WEEK

47

Month(s) _____

Monday the _____

7 AM	2
8	3
9	4
10	5
11	6
NOON	7
1 PM	8

Tuesday the _____

7 AM	2
8	3
9	4
10	5
11	6
NOON	7
1 PM	8

Wednesday the _____

7 AM	2
8	3
9	4
10	5
11	6
NOON	7
1 PM	8

WEEK

48

Week No. _____

Thursday the _____

7 AM	2
8	3
9	4
10	5
11	6
NOON	7
1 PM	8

Friday the _____

7 AM	2
8	3
9	4
10	5
11	6
NOON	7
1 PM	8

Saturday the _____ Sunday the _____

7 AM	2	7 AM	2
8	3	8	3
9	4	9	4
10	5	10	5
11	6	11	6
NOON	7	NOON	7
1 PM	8	1 PM	8

Month(s) _____

Monday the _____

7 AM	2
8	3
9	4
10	5
11	6
NOON	7
1 PM	8

Tuesday the _____

7 AM	2
8	3
9	4
10	5
11	6
NOON	7
1 PM	8

Wednesday the _____

7 AM	2
8	3
9	4
10	5
11	6
NOON	7
1 PM	8

WEEK

Week No. _____

Thursday the _____

7 AM	2
8	3
9	4
10	5
11	6
NOON	7
1 PM	8

Friday the _____

7 AM	2
8	3
9	4
10	5
11	6
NOON	7
1 PM	8

Saturday the _____

7 AM	2
8	3
9	4
10	5
11	6
NOON	7
1 PM	8

Sunday the _____

7 AM	2
8	3
9	4
10	5
11	6
NOON	7
1 PM	8

WEEK

51

Month(s) ―――――――――――――――――――――

Monday the ―――――――――――

7 AM	2
8	3
9	4
10	5
11	6
NOON	7
1 PM	8

Tuesday the ―――――――――――

7 AM	2
8	3
9	4
10	5
11	6
NOON	7
1 PM	8

Wednesday the ―――――――――――

7 AM	2
8	3
9	4
10	5
11	6
NOON	7
1 PM	8

Week No. _____

Thursday the _____

7 AM	2
8	3
9	4
10	5
11	6
NOON	7
1 PM	8

Friday the _____

7 AM	2
8	3
9	4
10	5
11	6
NOON	7
1 PM	8

Saturday the _____   Sunday the _____

7 AM	2		7 AM	2
8	3		8	3
9	4		9	4
10	5		10	5
11	6		11	6
NOON	7		NOON	7
1 PM	8		1 PM	8

WEEK

53

Month(s) _____

Monday the _____

7 AM	2
8	3
9	4
10	5
11	6
NOON	7
1 PM	8

Tuesday the _____

7 AM	2
8	3
9	4
10	5
11	6
NOON	7
1 PM	8

Wednesday the _____

7 AM	2
8	3
9	4
10	5
11	6
NOON	7
1 PM	8

WEEK

Week No. _____

Thursday the _____

7 AM	2
8	3
9	4
10	5
11	6
NOON	7
1 PM	8

Friday the _____

7 AM	2
8	3
9	4
10	5
11	6
NOON	7
1 PM	8

Saturday the _____   Sunday the _____

7 AM	2		7 AM	2
8	3		8	3
9	4		9	4
10	5		10	5
11	6		11	6
NOON	7		NOON	7
1 PM	8		1 PM	8

WEEK

55

Month(s) _____

Monday the _____

7 AM	2
8	3
9	4
10	5
11	6
NOON	7
1 PM	8

Tuesday the _____

7 AM	2
8	3
9	4
10	5
11	6
NOON	7
1 PM	8

Wednesday the _____

7 AM	2
8	3
9	4
10	5
11	6
NOON	7
1 PM	8

WEEK

Week No. _____

Thursday the _____

7 AM	2
8	3
9	4
10	5
11	6
NOON	7
1 PM	8

Friday the _____

7 AM	2
8	3
9	4
10	5
11	6
NOON	7
1 PM	8

Saturday the _____

7 AM	2
8	3
9	4
10	5
11	6
NOON	7
1 PM	8

Sunday the _____

7 AM	2
8	3
9	4
10	5
11	6
NOON	7
1 PM	8

Month(s) ———————————————————

Monday the ————————————

7 AM	*2*
8	*3*
9	*4*
10	*5*
11	*6*
Noon	*7*
1 PM	*8*

Tuesday the ————————————

7 AM	*2*
8	*3*
9	*4*
10	*5*
11	*6*
Noon	*7*
1 PM	*8*

Wednesday the ————————————

7 AM	*2*
8	*3*
9	*4*
10	*5*
11	*6*
Noon	*7*
1 PM	*8*

58

Week No. _____

Thursday the _____

7 AM	2
8	3
9	4
10	5
11	6
NOON	7
1 PM	8

Friday the _____

7 AM	2
8	3
9	4
10	5
11	6
NOON	7
1 PM	8

Saturday the _____ Sunday the _____

7 AM	2	7 AM	2
8	3	8	3
9	4	9	4
10	5	10	5
11	6	11	6
NOON	7	NOON	7
1 PM	8	1 PM	8

Month(s) ─────────────────────────────

Monday the ────────────────

7 AM	2
8	3
9	4
10	5
11	6
NOON	7
1 PM	8

Tuesday the ────────────────

7 AM	2
8	3
9	4
10	5
11	6
NOON	7
1 PM	8

Wednesday the ────────────────

7 AM	2
8	3
9	4
10	5
11	6
NOON	7
1 PM	8

WEEK

Week No. _____

Thursday the _____

7 AM	2
8	3
9	4
10	5
11	6
NOON	7
1 PM	8

Friday the _____

7 AM	2
8	3
9	4
10	5
11	6
NOON	7
1 PM	8

Saturday the _____ Sunday the _____

7 AM	2	7 AM	2
8	3	8	3
9	4	9	4
10	5	10	5
11	6	11	6
NOON	7	NOON	7
1 PM	8	1 PM	8

61

Month(s) _____

Monday the _____

7 AM	2
8	3
9	4
10	5
11	6
NOON	7
1 PM	8

Tuesday the _____

7 AM	2
8	3
9	4
10	5
11	6
NOON	7
1 PM	8

Wednesday the _____

7 AM	2
8	3
9	4
10	5
11	6
NOON	7
1 PM	8

Week No. _____

Thursday the _____

7 AM	2
8	3
9	4
10	5
11	6
NOON	7
1 PM	8

Friday the _____

7 AM	2
8	3
9	4
10	5
11	6
NOON	7
1 PM	8

Saturday the _____   Sunday the _____

7 AM	2	7 AM	2
8	3	8	3
9	4	9	4
10	5	10	5
11	6	11	6
NOON	7	NOON	7
1 PM	8	1 PM	8

WEEK

63

Month(s) _____

Monday the _____

7 AM	2
8	3
9	4
10	5
11	6
NOON	7
1 PM	8

Tuesday the _____

7 AM	2
8	3
9	4
10	5
11	6
NOON	7
1 PM	8

Wednesday the _____

7 AM	2
8	3
9	4
10	5
11	6
NOON	7
1 PM	8

Week No. _____

Thursday the _____

7 AM	2
8	3
9	4
10	5
11	6
NOON	7
1 PM	8

Friday the _____

7 AM	2
8	3
9	4
10	5
11	6
NOON	7
1 PM	8

Saturday the _____   Sunday the _____

7 AM	2	7 AM	2
8	3	8	3
9	4	9	4
10	5	10	5
11	6	11	6
NOON	7	NOON	7
1 PM	8	1 PM	8

WEEK

65

Month(s) ——————————————————————

Monday the —————————

7 AM	2
8	3
9	4
10	5
11	6
NOON	7
1 PM	8

Tuesday the —————————

7 AM	2
8	3
9	4
10	5
11	6
NOON	7
1 PM	8

Wednesday the —————————

7 AM	2
8	3
9	4
10	5
11	6
NOON	7
1 PM	8

Week No. _____

Thursday the _____

7 AM	2
8	3
9	4
10	5
11	6
NOON	7
1 PM	8

Friday the _____

7 AM	2
8	3
9	4
10	5
11	6
NOON	7
1 PM	8

Saturday the _____ Sunday the _____

7 AM	2	7 AM	2
8	3	8	3
9	4	9	4
10	5	10	5
11	6	11	6
NOON	7	NOON	7
1 PM	8	1 PM	8

Month(s) ────────────────────────

Monday the ─────────────

7 AM	2
8	3
9	4
10	5
11	6
NOON	7
1 PM	8

Tuesday the ─────────────

7 AM	2
8	3
9	4
10	5
11	6
NOON	7
1 PM	8

Wednesday the ─────────────

7 AM	2
8	3
9	4
10	5
11	6
NOON	7
1 PM	8

WEEK

68

Week No. _____

Thursday the _____

7 AM	2
8	3
9	4
10	5
11	6
NOON	7
1 PM	8

Friday the _____

7 AM	2
8	3
9	4
10	5
11	6
NOON	7
1 PM	8

Saturday the _____   Sunday the _____

7 AM	2	7 AM	2
8	3	8	3
9	4	9	4
10	5	10	5
11	6	11	6
NOON	7	NOON	7
1 PM	8	1 PM	8

Month(s) ─────────────────────

Monday the ────────────────

7 AM	2
8	3
9	4
10	5
11	6
NOON	7
1 PM	8

Tuesday the ────────────────

7 AM	2
8	3
9	4
10	5
11	6
NOON	7
1 PM	8

Wednesday the ────────────────

7 AM	2
8	3
9	4
10	5
11	6
NOON	7
1 PM	8

WEEK

70

Thursday the ──────────────

7 AM	2
8	3
9	4
10	5
11	6
NOON	7
1 PM	8

Friday the ──────────────

7 AM	2
8	3
9	4
10	5
11	6
NOON	7
1 PM	8

Saturday the ──────────────

7 AM	2
8	3
9	4
10	5
11	6
NOON	7
1 PM	8

Sunday the ──────────────

7 AM	2
8	3
9	4
10	5
11	6
NOON	7
1 PM	8

WEEK

71

Month(s) _____

Monday the _____

7 AM	2
8	3
9	4
10	5
11	6
NOON	7
1 PM	8

Tuesday the _____

7 AM	2
8	3
9	4
10	5
11	6
NOON	7
1 PM	8

Wednesday the _____

7 AM	2
8	3
9	4
10	5
11	6
NOON	7
1 PM	8

Week No. _____

Thursday the _____

7 AM	*2*
8	*3*
9	*4*
10	*5*
11	*6*
NOON	*7*
1 PM	*8*

Friday the _____

7 AM	*2*
8	*3*
9	*4*
10	*5*
11	*6*
NOON	*7*
1 PM	*8*

Saturday the _____   Sunday the _____

7 AM	*2*	*7 AM*	*2*
8	*3*	*8*	*3*
9	*4*	*9*	*4*
10	*5*	*10*	*5*
11	*6*	*11*	*6*
NOON	*7*	*NOON*	*7*
1 PM	*8*	*1 PM*	*8*

Month(s) _____

Monday the _____

7 AM	2
8	3
9	4
10	5
11	6
NOON	7
1 PM	8

Tuesday the _____

7 AM	2
8	3
9	4
10	5
11	6
NOON	7
1 PM	8

Wednesday the _____

7 AM	2
8	3
9	4
10	5
11	6
NOON	7
1 PM	8

Week No. _____

Thursday the _____

7 AM	2
8	3
9	4
10	5
11	6
Noon	7
1 PM	8

Friday the _____

7 AM	2
8	3
9	4
10	5
11	6
Noon	7
1 PM	8

Saturday the _____　　Sunday the _____

7 AM	2	7 AM	2
8	3	8	3
9	4	9	4
10	5	10	5
11	6	11	6
Noon	7	Noon	7
1 PM	8	1 PM	8

Month(s) _____

Monday the _____

7 AM	2
8	3
9	4
10	5
11	6
NOON	7
1 PM	8

Tuesday the _____

7 AM	2
8	3
9	4
10	5
11	6
NOON	7
1 PM	8

Wednesday the _____

7 AM	2
8	3
9	4
10	5
11	6
NOON	7
1 PM	8

Week No. _____

Thursday the _____

7 AM	2
8	3
9	4
10	5
11	6
NOON	7
1 PM	8

Friday the _____

7 AM	2
8	3
9	4
10	5
11	6
NOON	7
1 PM	8

Saturday the _____   Sunday the _____

7 AM	2	7 AM	2
8	3	8	3
9	4	9	4
10	5	10	5
11	6	11	6
NOON	7	NOON	7
1 PM	8	1 PM	8

WEEK

77

Month(s) _____

Monday the _____

7 AM	2
8	3
9	4
10	5
11	6
NOON	7
1 PM	8

Tuesday the _____

7 AM	2
8	3
9	4
10	5
11	6
NOON	7
1 PM	8

Wednesday the _____

7 AM	2
8	3
9	4
10	5
11	6
NOON	7
1 PM	8

WEEK

Week No. _____

Thursday the _____

7 AM	2
8	3
9	4
10	5
11	6
Noon	7
1 PM	8

Friday the _____

7 AM	2
8	3
9	4
10	5
11	6
Noon	7
1 PM	8

Saturday the _____   Sunday the _____

7 AM	2	7 AM	2
8	3	8	3
9	4	9	4
10	5	10	5
11	6	11	6
Noon	7	Noon	7
1 PM	8	1 PM	8

Month(s) ───────────────────────────

Monday the ─────────────────

7 AM	2
8	3
9	4
10	5
11	6
NOON	7
1 PM	8

Tuesday the ─────────────────

7 AM	2
8	3
9	4
10	5
11	6
NOON	7
1 PM	8

Wednesday the ─────────────────

7 AM	2
8	3
9	4
10	5
11	6
NOON	7
1 PM	8

WEEK

80

Week No. _____

Thursday the _____

7 AM	2
8	3
9	4
10	5
11	6
Noon	7
1 PM	8

Friday the _____

7 AM	2
8	3
9	4
10	5
11	6
Noon	7
1 PM	8

Saturday the _____

7 AM	2
8	3
9	4
10	5
11	6
Noon	7
1 PM	8

Sunday the _____

7 AM	2
8	3
9	4
10	5
11	6
Noon	7
1 PM	8

WEEK

Month(s) —————————————————————

Monday the —————————

7 AM	2
8	3
9	4
10	5
11	6
NOON	7
1 PM	8

Tuesday the —————————

7 AM	2
8	3
9	4
10	5
11	6
NOON	7
1 PM	8

Wednesday the —————————

7 AM	2
8	3
9	4
10	5
11	6
NOON	7
1 PM	8

Week No. _____

Thursday the _____

7 AM	2
8	3
9	4
10	5
11	6
NOON	7
1 PM	8

Friday the _____

7 AM	2
8	3
9	4
10	5
11	6
NOON	7
1 PM	8

Saturday the _____   Sunday the _____

7 AM	2	7 AM	2
8	3	8	3
9	4	9	4
10	5	10	5
11	6	11	6
NOON	7	NOON	7
1 PM	8	1 PM	8

WEEK

83

Month(s) ———————————————

Monday the ——————————

7 AM	2
8	3
9	4
10	5
11	6
NOON	7
1 PM	8

Tuesday the ——————————

7 AM	2
8	3
9	4
10	5
11	6
NOON	7
1 PM	8

Wednesday the ——————————

7 AM	2
8	3
9	4
10	5
11	6
NOON	7
1 PM	8

WEEK

84

Thursday the _____

7 AM	2
8	3
9	4
10	5
11	6
NOON	7
1 PM	8

Friday the _____

7 AM	2
8	3
9	4
10	5
11	6
NOON	7
1 PM	8

Saturday the _____ **Sunday the** _____

7 AM	2	7 AM	2
8	3	8	3
9	4	9	4
10	5	10	5
11	6	11	6
NOON	7	NOON	7
1 PM	8	1 PM	8

WEEK

85

Month(s) _____

Monday the _____

7 AM	2
8	3
9	4
10	5
11	6
NOON	7
1 PM	8

Tuesday the _____

7 AM	2
8	3
9	4
10	5
11	6
NOON	7
1 PM	8

Wednesday the _____

7 AM	2
8	3
9	4
10	5
11	6
NOON	7
1 PM	8

Week No. _____

Thursday the _____

7 AM	2
8	3
9	4
10	5
11	6
NOON	7
1 PM	8

Friday the _____

7 AM	2
8	3
9	4
10	5
11	6
NOON	7
1 PM	8

Saturday the _____

7 AM	2
8	3
9	4
10	5
11	6
NOON	7
1 PM	8

Sunday the _____

7 AM	2
8	3
9	4
10	5
11	6
NOON	7
1 PM	8

Month(s) _____

Monday the _____

7 AM	2
8	3
9	4
10	5
11	6
NOON	7
1 PM	8

Tuesday the _____

7 AM	2
8	3
9	4
10	5
11	6
NOON	7
1 PM	8

Wednesday the _____

7 AM	2
8	3
9	4
10	5
11	6
NOON	7
1 PM	8

Week No. _____

Thursday the _____

7 AM	2
8	3
9	4
10	5
11	6
NOON	7
1 PM	8

Friday the _____

7 AM	2
8	3
9	4
10	5
11	6
NOON	7
1 PM	8

Saturday the _____   Sunday the _____

7 AM	2	7 AM	2
8	3	8	3
9	4	9	4
10	5	10	5
11	6	11	6
NOON	7	NOON	7
1 PM	8	1 PM	8

Month(s) ————————————————

Monday the ————————

7 AM	2
8	3
9	4
10	5
11	6
NOON	7
1 PM	8

Tuesday the ————————

7 AM	2
8	3
9	4
10	5
11	6
NOON	7
1 PM	8

Wednesday the ————————

7 AM	2
8	3
9	4
10	5
11	6
NOON	7
1 PM	8

Week No. _____

Thursday the _____

7 AM	2
8	3
9	4
10	5
11	6
NOON	7
1 PM	8

Friday the _____

7 AM	2
8	3
9	4
10	5
11	6
NOON	7
1 PM	8

Saturday the _____   Sunday the _____

7 AM	2	7 AM	2
8	3	8	3
9	4	9	4
10	5	10	5
11	6	11	6
NOON	7	NOON	7
1 PM	8	1 PM	8

Month(s) _____

Monday the _____

7 AM	2
8	3
9	4
10	5
11	6
NOON	7
1 PM	8

Tuesday the _____

7 AM	2
8	3
9	4
10	5
11	6
NOON	7
1 PM	8

Wednesday the _____

7 AM	2
8	3
9	4
10	5
11	6
NOON	7
1 PM	8

Thursday the _____

7 AM	2
8	3
9	4
10	5
11	6
NOON	7
1 PM	8

Friday the _____

7 AM	2
8	3
9	4
10	5
11	6
NOON	7
1 PM	8

Saturday the _____ **Sunday the** _____

7 AM	2	7 AM	2
8	3	8	3
9	4	9	4
10	5	10	5
11	6	11	6
NOON	7	NOON	7
1 PM	8	1 PM	8

WEEK

93

Month(s) _____

Monday the _____

7 AM	2
8	3
9	4
10	5
11	6
NOON	7
1 PM	8

Tuesday the _____

7 AM	2
8	3
9	4
10	5
11	6
NOON	7
1 PM	8

Wednesday the _____

7 AM	2
8	3
9	4
10	5
11	6
NOON	7
1 PM	8

Week No. _____

Thursday the _____

7 AM	2
8	3
9	4
10	5
11	6
Noon	7
1 PM	8

Friday the _____

7 AM	2
8	3
9	4
10	5
11	6
Noon	7
1 PM	8

Saturday the _____

7 AM	2
8	3
9	4
10	5
11	6
Noon	7
1 PM	8

Sunday the _____

7 AM	2
8	3
9	4
10	5
11	6
Noon	7
1 PM	8

WEEK

Month(s) _____

Monday the _____

7 AM	2
8	3
9	4
10	5
11	6
NOON	7
1 PM	8

Tuesday the _____

7 AM	2
8	3
9	4
10	5
11	6
NOON	7
1 PM	8

Wednesday the _____

7 AM	2
8	3
9	4
10	5
11	6
NOON	7
1 PM	8

Week No. _____

Thursday the _____

7 AM	2
8	3
9	4
10	5
11	6
NOON	7
1 PM	8

Friday the _____

7 AM	2
8	3
9	4
10	5
11	6
NOON	7
1 PM	8

Saturday the _____ **Sunday the** _____

7 AM	2	7 AM	2
8	3	8	3
9	4	9	4
10	5	10	5
11	6	11	6
NOON	7	NOON	7
1 PM	8	1 PM	8

Month(s) _____

Monday the _____

7 AM	2
8	3
9	4
10	5
11	6
NOON	7
1 PM	8

Tuesday the _____

7 AM	2
8	3
9	4
10	5
11	6
NOON	7
1 PM	8

Wednesday the _____

7 AM	2
8	3
9	4
10	5
11	6
NOON	7
1 PM	8

WEEK

Week No. _____

Thursday the _____

7 AM	2
8	3
9	4
10	5
11	6
NOON	7
1 PM	8

Friday the _____

7 AM	2
8	3
9	4
10	5
11	6
NOON	7
1 PM	8

Saturday the _____

7 AM	2
8	3
9	4
10	5
11	6
NOON	7
1 PM	8

Sunday the _____

7 AM	2
8	3
9	4
10	5
11	6
NOON	7
1 PM	8

Month(s) —

Monday the —

7 AM	2
8	3
9	4
10	5
11	6
NOON	7
1 PM	8

Tuesday the —

7 AM	2
8	3
9	4
10	5
11	6
NOON	7
1 PM	8

Wednesday the —

7 AM	2
8	3
9	4
10	5
11	6
NOON	7
1 PM	8

WEEK

100

Week No. _____

Thursday the _____

7 AM	2
8	3
9	4
10	5
11	6
NOON	7
1 PM	8

Friday the _____

7 AM	2
8	3
9	4
10	5
11	6
NOON	7
1 PM	8

Saturday the _____

7 AM	2
8	3
9	4
10	5
11	6
NOON	7
1 PM	8

Sunday the _____

7 AM	2
8	3
9	4
10	5
11	6
NOON	7
1 PM	8

Month(s) _____

Monday the _____

7 AM	2
8	3
9	4
10	5
11	6
NOON	7
1 PM	8

Tuesday the _____

7 AM	2
8	3
9	4
10	5
11	6
NOON	7
1 PM	8

Wednesday the _____

7 AM	2
8	3
9	4
10	5
11	6
NOON	7
1 PM	8

Week No. _____

Thursday the _____

7 AM	2
8	3
9	4
10	5
11	6
NOON	7
1 PM	8

Friday the _____

7 AM	2
8	3
9	4
10	5
11	6
NOON	7
1 PM	8

Saturday the _____   **Sunday the** _____

7 AM	2	7 AM	2
8	3	8	3
9	4	9	4
10	5	10	5
11	6	11	6
NOON	7	NOON	7
1 PM	8	1 PM	8

103

Month(s) _____

Monday the _____

7 AM		2	
8		3	
9		4	
10		5	
11		6	
NOON		7	
1 PM		8	

Tuesday the _____

7 AM		2	
8		3	
9		4	
10		5	
11		6	
NOON		7	
1 PM		8	

Wednesday the _____

7 AM		2	
8		3	
9		4	
10		5	
11		6	
NOON		7	
1 PM		8	

Week No. _____

Thursday the _____

7 AM	2
8	3
9	4
10	5
11	6
NOON	7
1 PM	8

Friday the _____

7 AM	2
8	3
9	4
10	5
11	6
NOON	7
1 PM	8

Saturday the _____   Sunday the _____

7 AM	2	7 AM	2
8	3	8	3
9	4	9	4
10	5	10	5
11	6	11	6
NOON	7	NOON	7
1 PM	8	1 PM	8

Month(s) _____

Monday the _____

7 AM	2
8	3
9	4
10	5
11	6
NOON	7
1 PM	8

Tuesday the _____

7 AM	2
8	3
9	4
10	5
11	6
NOON	7
1 PM	8

Wednesday the _____

7 AM	2
8	3
9	4
10	5
11	6
NOON	7
1 PM	8

Week No. _____

Thursday the _____

7 AM	2
8	3
9	4
10	5
11	6
NOON	7
1 PM	8

Friday the _____

7 AM	2
8	3
9	4
10	5
11	6
NOON	7
1 PM	8

Saturday the _____

7 AM	2
8	3
9	4
10	5
11	6
NOON	7
1 PM	8

Sunday the _____

7 AM	2
8	3
9	4
10	5
11	6
NOON	7
1 PM	8

WEEK

107

Month(s) _____

Monday the _____

7 AM	2
8	3
9	4
10	5
11	6
NOON	7
1 PM	8

Tuesday the _____

7 AM	2
8	3
9	4
10	5
11	6
NOON	7
1 PM	8

Wednesday the _____

7 AM	2
8	3
9	4
10	5
11	6
NOON	7
1 PM	8

Week No. _____

Thursday the _____

7 AM	2
8	3
9	4
10	5
11	6
NOON	7
1 PM	8

Friday the _____

7 AM	2
8	3
9	4
10	5
11	6
NOON	7
1 PM	8

Saturday the _____

7 AM	2
8	3
9	4
10	5
11	6
NOON	7
1 PM	8

Sunday the _____

7 AM	2
8	3
9	4
10	5
11	6
NOON	7
1 PM	8

Month(s) _____

Monday the _____

7 AM	2
8	3
9	4
10	5
11	6
NOON	7
1 PM	8

Tuesday the _____

7 AM	2
8	3
9	4
10	5
11	6
NOON	7
1 PM	8

Wednesday the _____

7 AM	2
8	3
9	4
10	5
11	6
NOON	7
1 PM	8

Week No. _____

Thursday the _____

7 AM	2
8	3
9	4
10	5
11	6
Noon	7
1 PM	8

Friday the _____

7 AM	2
8	3
9	4
10	5
11	6
Noon	7
1 PM	8

Saturday the _____ Sunday the _____

7 AM	2	7 AM	2
8	3	8	3
9	4	9	4
10	5	10	5
11	6	11	6
Noon	7	Noon	7
1 PM	8	1 PM	8

111

Month(s) —————————————————————————

Monday the —————————————

7 AM	2
8	3
9	4
10	5
11	6
NOON	7
1 PM	8

Tuesday the —————————————

7 AM	2
8	3
9	4
10	5
11	6
NOON	7
1 PM	8

Wednesday the —————————————

7 AM	2
8	3
9	4
10	5
11	6
NOON	7
1 PM	8

Week No. _____

Thursday the _____

7 AM	2
8	3
9	4
10	5
11	6
NOON	7
1 PM	8

Friday the _____

7 AM	2
8	3
9	4
10	5
11	6
NOON	7
1 PM	8

Saturday the _____   Sunday the _____

7 AM	2	7 AM	2
8	3	8	3
9	4	9	4
10	5	10	5
11	6	11	6
NOON	7	NOON	7
1 PM	8	1 PM	8

Month(s) _____

Monday the _____

7 AM	2
8	3
9	4
10	5
11	6
NOON	7
1 PM	8

Tuesday the _____

7 AM	2
8	3
9	4
10	5
11	6
NOON	7
1 PM	8

Wednesday the _____

7 AM	2
8	3
9	4
10	5
11	6
NOON	7
1 PM	8

Week No. _____

Thursday the _____

7 AM	2
8	3
9	4
10	5
11	6
NOON	7
1 PM	8

Friday the _____

7 AM	2
8	3
9	4
10	5
11	6
NOON	7
1 PM	8

Saturday the _____ Sunday the _____

7 AM	2	7 AM	2
8	3	8	3
9	4	9	4
10	5	10	5
11	6	11	6
NOON	7	NOON	7
1 PM	8	1 PM	8

WEEK

115

Month(s) ———————————————————

Monday the ———————————

7 AM	2
8	3
9	4
10	5
11	6
NOON	7
1 PM	8

Tuesday the ———————————

7 AM	2
8	3
9	4
10	5
11	6
NOON	7
1 PM	8

Wednesday the ———————————

7 AM	2
8	3
9	4
10	5
11	6
NOON	7
1 PM	8

Week No. _____

Thursday the _____

7 AM	2
8	3
9	4
10	5
11	6
NOON	7
1 PM	8

Friday the _____

7 AM	2
8	3
9	4
10	5
11	6
NOON	7
1 PM	8

Saturday the _____ Sunday the _____

7 AM	2	7 AM	2
8	3	8	3
9	4	9	4
10	5	10	5
11	6	11	6
NOON	7	NOON	7
1 PM	8	1 PM	8

WEEK

117

Month(s) ―――――――――――――――――――

Monday the ――――――――

7 AM	2
8	3
9	4
10	5
11	6
NOON	7
1 PM	8

Tuesday the ――――――――

7 AM	2
8	3
9	4
10	5
11	6
NOON	7
1 PM	8

Wednesday the ――――――――

7 AM	2
8	3
9	4
10	5
11	6
NOON	7
1 PM	8

118

Week No. _____

Thursday the _____

7 AM	2
8	3
9	4
10	5
11	6
NOON	7
1 PM	8

Friday the _____

7 AM	2
8	3
9	4
10	5
11	6
NOON	7
1 PM	8

Saturday the _____   Sunday the _____

7 AM	2	7 AM	2
8	3	8	3
9	4	9	4
10	5	10	5
11	6	11	6
NOON	7	NOON	7
1 PM	8	1 PM	8

WEEK

119

Month(s) _____

Monday the _____

7 AM	2
8	3
9	4
10	5
11	6
NOON	7
1 PM	8

Tuesday the _____

7 AM	2
8	3
9	4
10	5
11	6
NOON	7
1 PM	8

Wednesday the _____

7 AM	2
8	3
9	4
10	5
11	6
NOON	7
1 PM	8

WEEK

Thursday the ———————————

7 AM	2
8	3
9	4
10	5
11	6
NOON	7
1 PM	8

Friday the ———————————

7 AM	2
8	3
9	4
10	5
11	6
NOON	7
1 PM	8

Saturday the ——————————— **Sunday the** ———————————

7 AM	2	7 AM	2
8	3	8	3
9	4	9	4
10	5	10	5
11	6	11	6
NOON	7	NOON	7
1 PM	8	1 PM	8

WEEK

121

Month(s)

Monday the

7 AM	2
8	3
9	4
10	5
11	6
NOON	7
1 PM	8

Tuesday the

7 AM	2
8	3
9	4
10	5
11	6
NOON	7
1 PM	8

Wednesday the

7 AM	2
8	3
9	4
10	5
11	6
NOON	7
1 PM	8

WEEK

122

Week No. _____

Thursday the _____

7 AM	2
8	3
9	4
10	5
11	6
NOON	7
1 PM	8

Friday the _____

7 AM	2
8	3
9	4
10	5
11	6
NOON	7
1 PM	8

Saturday the _____   Sunday the _____

7 AM	2	7 AM	2
8	3	8	3
9	4	9	4
10	5	10	5
11	6	11	6
NOON	7	NOON	7
1 PM	8	1 PM	8

Month(s) _____

Monday the _____

7 AM	2
8	3
9	4
10	5
11	6
NOON	7
1 PM	8

Tuesday the _____

7 AM	2
8	3
9	4
10	5
11	6
NOON	7
1 PM	8

Wednesday the _____

7 AM	2
8	3
9	4
10	5
11	6
NOON	7
1 PM	8

Week No. _____

Thursday the _____

7 AM	2
8	3
9	4
10	5
11	6
NOON	7
1 PM	8

Friday the _____

7 AM	2
8	3
9	4
10	5
11	6
NOON	7
1 PM	8

Saturday the _____

7 AM	2
8	3
9	4
10	5
11	6
NOON	7
1 PM	8

Sunday the _____

7 AM	2
8	3
9	4
10	5
11	6
NOON	7
1 PM	8

Month(s) ⎯⎯⎯⎯⎯⎯⎯⎯⎯⎯⎯⎯⎯⎯⎯⎯⎯⎯⎯

Monday the ⎯⎯⎯⎯⎯⎯⎯⎯

7 AM	2
8	3
9	4
10	5
11	6
NOON	7
1 PM	8

Tuesday the ⎯⎯⎯⎯⎯⎯⎯⎯

7 AM	2
8	3
9	4
10	5
11	6
NOON	7
1 PM	8

Wednesday the ⎯⎯⎯⎯⎯⎯⎯⎯

7 AM	2
8	3
9	4
10	5
11	6
NOON	7
1 PM	8

Week No. _____

Thursday the _____

7 AM	2
8	3
9	4
10	5
11	6
NOON	7
1 PM	8

Friday the _____

7 AM	2
8	3
9	4
10	5
11	6
NOON	7
1 PM	8

Saturday the _____ Sunday the _____

7 AM	2	7 AM	2
8	3	8	3
9	4	9	4
10	5	10	5
11	6	11	6
NOON	7	NOON	7
1 PM	8	1 PM	8

Month(s) ―――――――――――――――――――――――

Monday the ――――――――――――――

7 AM	2
8	3
9	4
10	5
11	6
NOON	7
1 PM	8

Tuesday the ――――――――――――――

7 AM	2
8	3
9	4
10	5
11	6
NOON	7
1 PM	8

Wednesday the ――――――――――――――

7 AM	2
8	3
9	4
10	5
11	6
NOON	7
1 PM	8

Week No. _____

Thursday the _____

7 AM	2
8	3
9	4
10	5
11	6
NOON	7
1 PM	8

Friday the _____

7 AM	2
8	3
9	4
10	5
11	6
NOON	7
1 PM	8

Saturday the _____

7 AM	2
8	3
9	4
10	5
11	6
NOON	7
1 PM	8

Sunday the _____

7 AM	2
8	3
9	4
10	5
11	6
NOON	7
1 PM	8

Month(s) _____

Monday the _____

7 AM	2
8	3
9	4
10	5
11	6
NOON	7
1 PM	8

Tuesday the _____

7 AM	2
8	3
9	4
10	5
11	6
NOON	7
1 PM	8

Wednesday the _____

7 AM	2
8	3
9	4
10	5
11	6
NOON	7
1 PM	8

Week No. _____

Thursday the _____

7 AM	2
8	3
9	4
10	5
11	6
NOON	7
1 PM	8

Friday the _____

7 AM	2
8	3
9	4
10	5
11	6
NOON	7
1 PM	8

Saturday the _____ | Sunday the _____

7 AM	2	7 AM	2
8	3	8	3
9	4	9	4
10	5	10	5
11	6	11	6
NOON	7	NOON	7
1 PM	8	1 PM	8

Month(s) _____

Monday the _____

7 AM	2
8	3
9	4
10	5
11	6
NOON	7
1 PM	8

Tuesday the _____

7 AM	2
8	3
9	4
10	5
11	6
NOON	7
1 PM	8

Wednesday the _____

7 AM	2
8	3
9	4
10	5
11	6
NOON	7
1 PM	8

WEEK

132

Week No. _____

Thursday the _____

7 AM	2
8	3
9	4
10	5
11	6
NOON	7
1 PM	8

Friday the _____

7 AM	2
8	3
9	4
10	5
11	6
NOON	7
1 PM	8

Saturday the _____ **Sunday the** _____

7 AM	2	7 AM	2
8	3	8	3
9	4	9	4
10	5	10	5
11	6	11	6
NOON	7	NOON	7
1 PM	8	1 PM	8

Month(s) _____

Monday the _____

7 AM	2
8	3
9	4
10	5
11	6
Noon	7
1 PM	8

Tuesday the _____

7 AM	2
8	3
9	4
10	5
11	6
Noon	7
1 PM	8

Wednesday the _____

7 AM	2
8	3
9	4
10	5
11	6
Noon	7
1 PM	8

Week No. _____

Thursday the _____

7 AM	2
8	3
9	4
10	5
11	6
NOON	7
1 PM	8

Friday the _____

7 AM	2
8	3
9	4
10	5
11	6
NOON	7
1 PM	8

Saturday the _____

7 AM	2
8	3
9	4
10	5
11	6
NOON	7
1 PM	8

Sunday the _____

7 AM	2
8	3
9	4
10	5
11	6
NOON	7
1 PM	8

Month(s) _____

Monday the _____

7 AM	2
8	3
9	4
10	5
11	6
Noon	7
1 PM	8

Tuesday the _____

7 AM	2
8	3
9	4
10	5
11	6
Noon	7
1 PM	8

Wednesday the _____

7 AM	2
8	3
9	4
10	5
11	6
Noon	7
1 PM	8

WEEK

Week No. _____

Thursday the _____

7 AM	2
8	3
9	4
10	5
11	6
NOON	7
1 PM	8

Friday the _____

7 AM	2
8	3
9	4
10	5
11	6
NOON	7
1 PM	8

Saturday the _____ Sunday the _____

7 AM	2	7 AM	2
8	3	8	3
9	4	9	4
10	5	10	5
11	6	11	6
NOON	7	NOON	7
1 PM	8	1 PM	8

Month(s) ————————————————————

Monday the ————————————

7 AM	2
8	3
9	4
10	5
11	6
NOON	7
1 PM	8

Tuesday the ————————————

7 AM	2
8	3
9	4
10	5
11	6
NOON	7
1 PM	8

Wednesday the ————————————

7 AM	2
8	3
9	4
10	5
11	6
NOON	7
1 PM	8

WEEK

138

Week No. ————————————————

Thursday the ————————————————

7 AM	2
8	3
9	4
10	5
11	6
Noon	7
1 PM	8

Friday the ————————————————

7 AM	2
8	3
9	4
10	5
11	6
Noon	7
1 PM	8

Saturday the ———————— Sunday the ————————

7 AM	2	7 AM	2
8	3	8	3
9	4	9	4
10	5	10	5
11	6	11	6
Noon	7	Noon	7
1 PM	8	1 PM	8

139

Month(s) ――――――――――――――――――――

Monday the ――――――――――

7 AM	2	
8	3	
9	4	
10	5	
11	6	
NOON	7	
1 PM	8	

Tuesday the ――――――――――

7 AM	2	
8	3	
9	4	
10	5	
11	6	
NOON	7	
1 PM	8	

Wednesday the ――――――――――

7 AM	2	
8	3	
9	4	
10	5	
11	6	
NOON	7	
1 PM	8	

Week No. _____

Thursday the _____

7 AM	2
8	3
9	4
10	5
11	6
NOON	7
1 PM	8

Friday the _____

7 AM	2
8	3
9	4
10	5
11	6
NOON	7
1 PM	8

Saturday the _____   Sunday the _____

7 AM	2	7 AM	2
8	3	8	3
9	4	9	4
10	5	10	5
11	6	11	6
NOON	7	NOON	7
1 PM	8	1 PM	8

Quick Guides
to College Success

"Success doesn't come to you; you go to it."

—Marva Collins (1936–),
educator

Note-Taking 1, 2, 3 . . .

Follow these guidelines to take effective notes.

1. Get Ready.

- Before class, do any reading or other assignments given by the instructor.

- Make sure to have pens or sharpened pencils ready.

- Prepare your note paper: At the top of the page, list the date, the class, and the topic that will be discussed. (Keep your notes for each class in separate notebooks or folders.)

2. Listen and Take Notes Actively.

- Listen to the instructor.

- Be selective instead of trying to write down every single word. Summarize as much as possible, and listen for words that signal key information, such as "This is important" or "You need to know this."

- Use abbreviations, such as *B4* for *before,* *w* for *with,* and *@* for *at.*

- If you have any questions about any topics covered by your instructor, ask him or her for clarification right away, and add these clarifications to your notes.

3. Review Your Notes.

- Review your notes as soon as possible after class, adding additional summaries or clarifications if necessary.

Quick and Dirty Tip from Get-It-Done Guy™

Add some color: Use multi-colored pens or high-lighters in class to signal important information as you take notes. You might put a big green exclamation point by reasons. Using different colors and even drawing pictures will engage your whole brain.

For a podcast on this subject, visit **getitdone .quickanddirtytips.com.** Topic: "Taking Killer Notes That Keep You on Top of Your Game"

- Make sample tests from your notes and put them aside. Then, take the sample tests before scheduled exams to check your knowledge of the information.

Studying for a Test 1, 2, 3 . . .

Follow these steps to be well prepared for any test.

1. Get Ready.

- Know what you need to study. If you are unclear about the priorities, ask your instructor.

- Give yourself enough study time, ideally during a time of day when you are most alert and ready to learn.

- Set aside a *regular* time to study. Even when you don't have a test, use this time to review course material and complete assignments.

- Don't wait until right before a test to study. The more you review the material, the more it will "sink in."

- Identify one or two serious, committed classmates to study with.

2. Study Effectively.

- Have all materials (notes, textbook, sample tests, etc.) ready in one spot. (Check to see if your textbook comes with a study guide, CD, or online resource that can help you prepare.)

- Go back through your notes, readings, and other study materials, highlighting and reviewing information important for the test.

- Use review checklists, chapter summaries, or other review materials in your textbook.

Quick and Dirty Tip from Get-It-Done Guy™

Summarize on one sheet: When preparing for a test, look over your notes and study materials, and summarize them on a single sheet of paper.

For a podcast on this subject, visit **getitdone .quickanddirtytips.com.** Topic: "Taking Killer Notes That Keep You on Top of Your Game"

- Make flash cards with important information and review these.

- Attend any study sessions offered by your instructor.

- Study with a classmate.

3. Test Your Knowledge.

- Answer questions on self-made practice tests or other practice tests.

- If you are studying with a classmate, quiz each other on the material.

Taking a Test 1, 2, 3 . . .

If you have studied for a test carefully and thoroughly (see page 145), you are well on your way to success! Right before the test, take the following steps to perform your best.

1. Get Ready.

- Get at least eight hours of sleep the night before the exam.

- Don't take a test on an empty stomach. Make sure that you've fueled your brain with a light, nutritious meal beforehand.

- Dress comfortably.

- Bring any required materials, such as pencils, pens, paper, or a calculator.

- Get to the test site early enough to get settled in. Take a deep breath and clear your mind so that you can focus on the test.

2. Use Smart Test-Taking Techniques.

- Listen to any spoken instructions, and read all written directions.

- Do the questions worth the most points first.

- Go to the questions that you definitely know the answers to. Sometimes, you can find answers to other questions this way.

- Finish the remaining questions; try not to leave anything unanswered.

- Keep track of time. If you are halfway through the test time but not halfway through the test, you may need to pick up your pace. On the other hand, try to stay calm, and don't move too fast.

- Do not change an answer unless you are 100% sure that you are changing it correctly.

- If you have time left over at the end, use it to review your work.

3. Review Your Returned Test and Learn from Your Mistakes.

- When you get back your test, look at answers that were marked as incorrect.

- Make sure that you know why each incorrect answer was marked as such. Consider these options:

  - I did not study the necessary information.

  - I misread the question.

  - I did not understand the question.

  - I did not answer the question completely.

- You might want to adjust your future studying and test-taking strategies to avoid these problems in the future.

Quick Grammar Guide

Proofread all of your papers carefully before turning them in for a grade. The following chart shows common grammar problems to look out for and how to solve them.

Problem(s)/Examples	Solution(s)/Examples
Fragments: Word groups (1) that are missing a subject ("who" or "what" a sentence is about) or a verb, or (2) that don't express a complete thought.	Join the fragment to a sentence before or after it.
Examples (fragments are underlined):	*Corrected examples:*
Mark and Danielle wanted to do only one thing. Go shopping.	Mark and Danielle wanted to do only one thing: go shopping.
Before I go to work. I run five miles.	Before I go to work, I run five miles.
To get to the bank. Turn right at the end of our street.	To get to the bank, turn right at the end of our street.
	Turn the fragment into a complete sentence.
	Corrected example:
	Mark and Danielle wanted to do only one thing. They wanted to shop every moment of the day.

Quick and Dirty Tip from Grammar Girl™

Test your writing for fragments: For each word group that looks like a sentence, ask if there is a verb. If there is no verb, you have a fragment. If there's a verb but no subject, ask if the word group is a command (*Run! Sit!*). If not, you have a fragment.

For a podcast on this subject, visit **grammar.quickanddirtytips.com.**
Topic: "Sentence Fragments"

Problem(s)/Examples	Solution(s)/Examples
Comma splice: Two sentences joined only by a comma. **Run-on (fused sentence):** Two sentences joined with no punctuation.	Separate the sentences with a comma and a coordinating conjunction (*and, but, for, nor, or, so, yet*).
Examples:	*Corrected example:*
Comma splice: Bill lost his job, he went on unemployment.	Bill lost his job, so he went on unemployment.
Run-on: Bill lost his job he went on unemployment.	**Use a semicolon (;) or period between the sentences.**
	Corrected examples:
Comma splice: I like steak, I like filet mignon better.	I like steak; I like filet mignon better.
Run-on: I like steak I like filet mignon better.	I like steak. I like filet mignon better.
	Use a subordinating conjunction (such as *although, after,* or *because*) at the start of one of the sentences.
	Corrected example:
Comma splice: Tina is smart, she was elected class president.	Because Tina is smart, she was elected class president.
Run-on: Tina is smart she was elected class president.	

Quick and Dirty Tip from Grammar Girl™

Remember your comma splice repair kit: It contains periods, semicolons, coordinating conjunctions, dashes, and colons. You can think of a semicolon as a "sentence splicer" because it splices complete sentences together.

For a podcast on this subject, visit **grammar .quickanddirtytips.com.** Topic: "Comma Splice"

Problem(s)/Examples	Solution(s)/Examples
Pronoun-antecedent agreement problems: When a pronoun does not agree with the word (antecedent) that it refers back to.	**Make both the pronoun and the antecedent singular.**
Examples of plural pronouns (their) *with singular antecedents* (anyone, company):	*Corrected examples:*
Anyone can improve their grades.	Anyone can improve his or her grades.
The company raised fees for their employees.	The company raised fees for its employees.
Note: Most indefinite pronouns (like *anyone, anything, everyone, somebody,* and *someone*) are singular. Often, collective nouns (like *company, jury,* and *team*) are also singular.	**Make both the pronoun and the antecedent plural.**
	Corrected example:
	All students can improve their grades.

Quick and Dirty Tip from Grammar Girl

Consider avoiding "he or she": Sometimes, writing "he or she" may be the only way to avoid an agreement problem. However, this expression can be awkward. Whenever possible, make subjects plural to avoid this problem. (*All students can improve their grades*).

For a podcast on this subject, visit **grammar.quickanddirtytips.com.** Topic: "Generic Singular Pronouns"

Problem(s)/Examples	Solution(s)/Examples
Subject-verb agreement problems: When a verb is not in the correct form to go with its subject: singular verbs with plural subjects and singlular verbs with plural subjects. *Examples of verbs that don't match their subjects:* Bob like fish. (singular subject; plural verb) The girls enjoys swimming. (plural subject; singular verb) **Note:** In the present tense, verbs with *he/she/it* subjects end in *–s* or *–es*.	**Make sure to use singular verbs with singular subjects and plural verbs with plural subjects.** *Corrected examples:* Bob likes fish. The girls enjoy swimming. Because verbs can be tricky, you might want to consult a writing text or handbook for more information.

Quick and Dirty Tip from Grammar Girl™

Look out for separated subjects and verbs: Errors tend to occur when the subject is far from the verb. Circle the word or words that form the subject, and ignore everything else.

Incorrect: The (use) of cell phones and pagers are prohibited.

Correct: The (use) of cell phones and pagers is prohibited.

For a podcast on this subject, visit **grammar .quickanddirtytips.com.** Topic: "Subject-Verb Agreement"

Address Book

" When we seek for connection, we restore the world to wholeness. Our seemingly separate lives become meaningful as we discover how truly necessary we are to each other. "

—Margaret Wheatley,
consultant and speaker

Address Book

Make sure to record useful school-related information, such as contact details for your instructors (and their office hours), for classmates you want to study with, and for other important people, such as tutors and learning center contacts.

Name: _____

Relationship: _____

(Instructor, study partner, tutor, etc.)

Address: _____

City: _____ State: _____ Zip: _____

Phone: _____ Fax: _____

E-mail: _____

Office hours (if instructor or tutor): _____

Name: _____

Relationship: _____

(Instructor, study partner, tutor, etc.)

Address: _____

City: _____ State: _____ Zip: _____

Phone: _____ Fax: _____

E-mail: _____

Office hours (if instructor or tutor): _____

Name: _____

Relationship: _____

(Instructor, study partner, tutor, etc.)

Address: _____

City: _____ State: _____ Zip: _____

Phone: _____ Fax: _____

E-mail: _____

Office hours (if instructor or tutor): _____

Name: _____

Relationship: _____

(Instructor, study partner, tutor, etc.)

Address: _____

City: _____ State: _____ Zip: _____

Phone: _____ Fax: _____

E-mail: _____

Office hours (if instructor or tutor): _____

Name: _____

Relationship: _____

(Instructor, study partner, tutor, etc.)

Address: _____

City: _____ State: _____ Zip: _____

Phone: _____ Fax: _____

E-mail: _____

Office hours (if instructor or tutor): _____

Quick and Dirty Tip from Get-It-Done Guy™

Label file folders smartly: Whether you store files in a cabinet or on your computer, avoid folder names that are too general ("Taking Over the World"); instead, use more specific labels (for example, one folder for each part of you plan for world domination). Later, you'll be able to find what you need more easily.

For a podcast on this subject, visit **getitdone.quickanddirtytips.com.** Topic: "Better Filing"

Name: _____

Relationship: _____

(Instructor, study partner, tutor, etc.)

Address: _____

City: _____ State: _____ Zip: _____

Phone: _____ Fax: _____

E-mail: _____

Office hours (if instructor or tutor): _____

Name: _____

Relationship: _____

(Instructor, study partner, tutor, etc.)

Address: _____

City: _____ State: _____ Zip: _____

Phone: _____ Fax: _____

E-mail: _____

Office hours (if instructor or tutor): _____

Name: _____

Relationship: _____

(Instructor, study partner, tutor, etc.)

Address: _____

City: _____ State: _____ Zip: _____

Phone: _____ Fax: _____

E-mail: _____

Office hours (if instructor or tutor): _____

Name: _____

Relationship: _____

(Instructor, study partner, tutor, etc.)

Address: _____

City: _____ State: _____ Zip: _____

Phone: _____ Fax: _____

E-mail: _____

Office hours (if instructor or tutor): _____

Name: _____

Relationship: _____

(Instructor, study partner, tutor, etc.)

Address: _____

City: _____ State: _____ Zip: _____

Phone: _____ Fax: _____

E-mail: _____

Office hours (if instructor or tutor): _____

Quick and Dirty Tip from Grammar Girl™

Remember to proofread: Typos and other errors are a problem for everyone—even professional writers! Don't forget to proofread your writing using these strategies: reading your work backwards, reading your work aloud, and reading a print-out of your writing (to pick up errors you might not notice on a computer screen).

For a podcast on this subject, visit **grammar.quickanddirtytips.com.** Topic: "Proofreading Tips"

Name: _____

Relationship: _____

(Instructor, study partner, tutor, etc.)

Address: _____

City: _____ State: _____ Zip: _____

Phone: _____ Fax: _____

E-mail: _____

Office hours (if instructor or tutor): _____

Name: _____

Relationship: _____

(Instructor, study partner, tutor, etc.)

Address: _____

City: _____ State: _____ Zip: _____

Phone: _____ Fax: _____

E-mail: _____

Office hours (if instructor or tutor): _____

Name: _____

Relationship: _____

(Instructor, study partner, tutor, etc.)

Address: _____

City: _____ State: _____ Zip: _____

Phone: _____ Fax: _____

E-mail: _____

Office hours (if instructor or tutor): _____

Name: _____

Relationship: _____

(Instructor, study partner, tutor, etc.)

Address: _____

City: _____ State: _____ Zip: _____

Phone: _____ Fax: _____

E-mail: _____

Office hours (if instructor or tutor): _____

Name: _____

Relationship: _____

(Instructor, study partner, tutor, etc.)

Address: _____

City: _____ State: _____ Zip: _____

Phone: _____ Fax: _____

E-mail: _____

Office hours (if instructor or tutor): _____

Name: _____

Relationship: _____

(Instructor, study partner, tutor, etc.)

Address: _____

City: _____ State: _____ Zip: _____

Phone: _____ Fax: _____

E-mail: _____

Office hours (if instructor or tutor): _____

Name: _____

Relationship: _____

(Instructor, study partner, tutor, etc.)

Address: _____

City: _____ State: _____ Zip: _____

Phone: _____ Fax: _____

E-mail: _____

Office hours (if instructor or tutor): _____

Name: _____

Relationship: _____

(Instructor, study partner, tutor, etc.)

Address: _____

City: _____ State: _____ Zip: _____

Phone: _____ Fax: _____

E-mail: _____

Office hours (if instructor or tutor): _____

Name: _____

Relationship: _____

(Instructor, study partner, tutor, etc.)

Address: _____

City: _____ State: _____ Zip: _____

Phone: _____ Fax: _____

E-mail: _____

Office hours (if instructor or tutor): _____

Name: _____

Relationship: _____

(Instructor, study partner, tutor, etc.)

Address: _____

City: _____ State: _____ Zip: _____

Phone: _____ Fax: _____

E-mail: _____

Office hours (if instructor or tutor): _____

Name: _____

Relationship: _____

(Instructor, study partner, tutor, etc.)

Address: _____

City: _____ State: _____ Zip: _____

Phone: _____ Fax: _____

E-mail: _____

Office hours (if instructor or tutor): _____

Name: _____

Relationship: _____

(Instructor, study partner, tutor, etc.)

Address: _____

City: _____ State: _____ Zip: _____

Phone: _____ Fax: _____

E-mail: _____

Office hours (if instructor or tutor): _____

Name: _____

Relationship: _____

(Instructor, study partner, tutor, etc.)

Address: _____

City: _____ State: _____ Zip: _____

Phone: _____ Fax: _____

E-mail: _____

Office hours (if instructor or tutor): _____

Name: _____

Relationship: _____

(Instructor, study partner, tutor, etc.)

Address: _____

City: _____ State: _____ Zip: _____

Phone: _____ Fax: _____

E-mail: _____

Office hours (if instructor or tutor): _____

Name: _____

Relationship: _____

(Instructor, study partner, tutor, etc.)

Address: _____

City: _____ State: _____ Zip: _____

Phone: _____ Fax: _____

E-mail: _____

Office hours (if instructor or tutor): _____

GUIDES

162

Name: _____

Relationship: _____

(Instructor, study partner, tutor, etc.)

Address: _____

City: _____ State: _____ Zip: _____

Phone: _____ Fax: _____

E-mail: _____

Office hours (if instructor or tutor): _____

Name: _____

Relationship: _____

(Instructor, study partner, tutor, etc.)

Address: _____

City: _____ State: _____ Zip: _____

Phone: _____ Fax: _____

E-mail: _____

Office hours (if instructor or tutor): _____

Name: _____

Relationship: _____

(Instructor, study partner, tutor, etc.)

Address: _____

City: _____ State: _____ Zip: _____

Phone: _____ Fax: _____

E-mail: _____

Office hours (if instructor or tutor): _____

163

Name: _____

Relationship: _____

(Instructor, study partner, tutor, etc.)

Address: _____

City: _____ State: _____ Zip: _____

Phone: _____ Fax: _____

E-mail: _____

Office hours (if instructor or tutor): _____

Name: _____

Relationship: _____

(Instructor, study partner, tutor, etc.)

Address: _____

City: _____ State: _____ Zip: _____

Phone: _____ Fax: _____

E-mail: _____

Office hours (if instructor or tutor): _____

Name: _____

Relationship: _____

(Instructor, study partner, tutor, etc.)

Address: _____

City: _____ State: _____ Zip: _____

Phone: _____ Fax: _____

E-mail: _____

Office hours (if instructor or tutor): _____

Name: _____

Relationship: _____

(Instructor, study partner, tutor, etc.)

Address: _____

City: _____ State: _____ Zip: _____

Phone: _____ Fax: _____

E-mail: _____

Office hours (if instructor or tutor): _____

Name: _____

Relationship: _____

(Instructor, study partner, tutor, etc.)

Address: _____

City: _____ State: _____ Zip: _____

Phone: _____ Fax: _____

E-mail: _____

Office hours (if instructor or tutor): _____

Name: _____

Relationship: _____

(Instructor, study partner, tutor, etc.)

Address: _____

City: _____ State: _____ Zip: _____

Phone: _____ Fax: _____

E-mail: _____

Office hours (if instructor or tutor): _____

Name: _____

Relationship: _____

(Instructor, study partner, tutor, etc.)

Address: _____

City: _____ State: _____ Zip: _____

Phone: _____ Fax: _____

E-mail: _____

Office hours (if instructor or tutor): _____

Name: _____

Relationship: _____

(Instructor, study partner, tutor, etc.)

Address: _____

City: _____ State: _____ Zip: _____

Phone: _____ Fax: _____

E-mail: _____

Office hours (if instructor or tutor): _____

Name: _____

Relationship: _____

(Instructor, study partner, tutor, etc.)

Address: _____

City: _____ State: _____ Zip: _____

Phone: _____ Fax: _____

E-mail: _____

Office hours (if instructor or tutor): _____

Notes

Selected Web Sites

Writing and Grammar Resources

Dictionary.com (http://dictionary.reference.com): An online dictionary.

Grammar Girl (http://grammar.quickanddirtytips.com): Friendly tips and podcasts to help you improve your grammar.

Guide to Grammar and Style (http://andromeda.rutgers.edu/ ~ jlynch/ Writing): Explanations of grammar and style topics and terms.

Howtostudy.org (http://www.howtostudy.org): Includes guidance on writing in different fields, as well as study advice and resources

Online English Grammar (http://edufind.com/english/grammar/toc.cfm): Explanations and examples of various grammar topics.

The Purdue Online Writing Lab (OWL) (http://owl.english.purdue.edu): Hundreds of resources related to writing, research, grammar and mechanics, and more.

Re:Writing Basics (http://bcs.bedfordstmartins.com/rewritingbasics): Writing and grammar exercises and tutorials, model paragraphs and essays, and more.

Writing in College: A Short Guide to College Writing by Joseph M. Williams and Lawrence McEnerney (http://writing-program.uchicago.edu/ resources/collegewriting): Offers guidance in responding to assignments; planning, drafting, and revising papers; working with writing tutors; and more.

Research and Documentation Resources

APAStyle.org (http://apastyle.org): Tips on using American Psychological Association (APA) documentation style. A style manual is published separately.

Internet Public Library (http://www.ipl.org): Online public library that collects research resources in different fields, provides online references, and more.

MLA Documentation (http://www.wisc.edu/writing/Handbook/DocMLA .html): Advice on creating parenthetical citations and works-cited pages according to Modern Language Association (MLA) style.